NEW BELIEVER

WORKBOOK & JOURNAL

Foundational Gospel Truths To Begin
Your Relationship With Christ Jesus.
Includes Journal Prompts To Go Deep

CHRISTINA PERERA

THIS BOOK BELONGS TO:

_____

CHRISTINA PERERA MINISTRIES

TABLE OF CONTENTS

Each section includes biblical teaching and journaling prompts to dive deep into God's Word, helping you begin an active prayer life.

We Have ALL Fallen Short.

But now the righteousness of God apart from the law is revealed, being witnessed by the Law and the Prophets, even the righteousness of God, through faith in Jesus Christ, to all and on all who believe. For there is no difference; for all have sinned and fall short of the glory of God, being justified freely by His grace through the redemption that is in Christ Jesus, whom God set forth as a propitiation by His blood, through faith, to demonstrate His righteousness, because in His forbearance God had passed over the sins that were previously committed, to demonstrate at the present time His righteousness, that He might be just and the justifier of the one who has faith in Jesus.

Romans 3:21-25 NKJV

THE LAW WAS GIVEN SO YOU WOULD SEE YOUR NEED FOR A SAVIOR.

From the beginning, men walked with God upon the earth, enjoying the sweetness of fellowship between a created being and its creator.

When the fall of man happened in Genesis, sin entered the world. For the first time, man became separated from God because of his sinful nature.

The Law of Moses was given on Mount Sinai to Moses, a mediator between God and the children of Israel, to communicate God's perfect standard of love.

The Law of Moses is the Ten Commandments which most of us know as a moral code. We're never designed to be used as justification for our righteousness.

The Bible clarifies that no man can stand before God and Justify himself. No matter what good you have done, there are still places you have fallen short.

But God So Loved the World!

Despite our human weakness and shameful failure to keep God's holy standard of love, God intervened on our behalf. The Father's love for the world is more significant than our sin and failures. He loves us so much that He sent His only son Jesus to become the sacrifice for our sins and lawless deeds. Before we could ever choose Him, He chose us.

LETS GO DEEP!

How does it make you feel knowing your heavenly Father sent His only Son despite your failure to keep His glorious standards?

_____

_____

_____

_____

_____

_____

WHERE HAVE YOU FALLEN SHORT OF GOD'S STANDARDS?

Pick a moment in your life or action where you know you have
fallen short of God's glorious standard of love.

_____

_____

_____

_____

_____

_____

_____

_____

_____

_____

_____

Invite Jesus into that moment and allow Him to speak to your
heart. Record what He is saying here.

_____

_____

_____

_____

_____

How did Jesus change that experience for you?

_____

_____

_____

_____

_____

_____

_____

_____

_____

_____

_____

_____

_____

_____

_____

_____

_____

_____

For *God*
so loved the world
HIS ONE AND ONLY SON
That whoever believes in Him shall not
perish but have ETERNAL LIFE.

John 3:16 NIV

What JESUS Has Done.

For I will be merciful to their unrighteousness, and their sins and their lawless deeds I will remember no more."
Hebrews 8:12 NKJV

CHRISTINA PERERA MINISTRIES

THE CROSS CHANGES EVERYTHING!

Under the Old Testament Law, God instituted a system of ceremonies, feasts, and sacrifices that would point the children of Israel to the coming Messiah.

God did not desire animal sacrifices but the ultimate sacrifice that would forever blot out the sins of the worshipers.

Each annual sacrifice pointed to an aspect of the coming Son. As the sin offering, Jesus completely absorbed all your sin, shame, and sickness at the cross.

He was resurrected without them. Therefore, you can be confident that your heavenly Father is satisfied with Jesus' work.

As a result, you can enjoy lasting peace with God and assurance that He will be gracious to you in time of need.

It Is Finished!

As a result of Jesus' perfect obedience to the will of the Father on the cross, we can rest assured that our sins and lawless deeds will be remembered no more!

Therefore, when He came into the world, He said: "Sacrifice and offering You did not desire, But a body You have prepared for Me.
Hebrews 10:5 NKJV

LETS GO DEEP!

Take a few moments and tell Jesus how grateful you are for His perfect sacrifice.

_____

_____

_____

_____

_____

_____

LETS GO DEEPER.

See your sin absorbed in the body of Jesus. How do you feel knowing your Heavenly Father will never remember your sins again?

_____

_____

_____

_____

_____

_____

See your shame absorbed in the body of Jesus. What does that mean to you? How can you live your life differently now?

_____

_____

_____

_____

_____

_____

_____

_____

_____

_____

See your sickness absorbed in the body of Jesus. What does that mean to you? How can you live differently now?

_____

_____

_____

_____

_____

_____

_____

_____

_____

_____

_____

_____

_____

_____

_____

_____

_____

For *God*
did not send his Son
into the world
to condemn the world
BUT TO SAVE THE WORLD
THROUGH HIM.

John 3:17 NIV

NEW Creation Life.

In Him you were also circumcised with the circumcision made without hands, by putting off the body of the sins of the flesh, by the circumcision of Christ, buried with Him in baptism, in which you also were raised with Him through faith in the working of God, who raised Him from the dead. And you, being dead in your trespasses and the uncircumcision of your flesh, He has made alive together with Him, having forgiven you all trespasses, having wiped out the handwriting of requirements that was against us, which was contrary to us. And He has taken it out of the way, having nailed it to the cross. Having disarmed principalities and powers, He made a public spectacle of them, triumphing over them in it.

Colossians 2:11-15 NKJV

YOU HAVE BEEN RAISED TO NEW LIFE IN CHRIST.

Your heavenly Father raised Christ from the grave by the power of the Holy Spirit.

Jesus rose without your sin, shame, and sickness. Therefore, you can be assured they do not belong to you anymore.

When Jesus rose, you rose with Him. He has been glorified and seated at the right hand of the Father far above all principality and power.

Jesus has restored the authority of man lost in the fall.

As a believer in Jesus, You have now been declared righteous by God, and His perfect righteousness has been transferred to your account.

Through your righteous standing before God, you now have the authority to bring the perfect reality of heaven into the earth.

CHRISTINA PERERA MINISTRIES

Seated In Christ.

But God, who is rich in mercy, because of His great love with which He loved us, even when we were dead in trespasses, made us alive together with Christ (by grace you have been saved), and raised us up together, and made us sit together in the heavenly places in Christ Jesus, that in the ages to come He might show the exceeding riches of His grace in His kindness toward us in Christ Jesus.

Ephesians 2:4-7 NKJV

LETS GO DEEP!

See yourself seated in Christ in heavenly places. What does that mean to you? How can you live differently now?

_____

_____

_____

_____

_____

_____

_____

LETS GO DEEPER.

Describe one area in your life that does not look like heaven.

_____

_____

_____

_____

_____

_____

Invite Jesus into that area and ask Him what He is saying about the situation. Record it here.

_____

_____

_____

_____

_____

_____

_____

_____

_____

Begin to declare what Jesus is speaking over your life. Record the results here.

_____

_____

_____

_____

_____

_____

_____

_____

_____

_____

_____

_____

_____

_____

_____

_____

_____

_____

Whoever believes in *Him* **IS NOT CONDEMNED,** but whoever does not believe stands condemned already because they have not believed **IN THE NAME OF GOD'S ONE AND ONLY SON.**

John 3:18 NIV

Relationship with JESUS.

And how shall they preach unless they are sent? As it is written: "How beautiful are the feet of those who preach the gospel of peace, Who bring glad tidings of good things!"

Romans 10:15 NKJV

CHRISTINA PERERA MINISTRIES

JESUS CONTINUALLY BRINGS GOOD NEWS

How beautiful are the feet that bring good news! Worshiping at the bottom of those nail-pierced feet who brought the news of the kingdom of God to Earth is one of my favorite places to be.

Our beloved King did not send an angel. He Himself came. He came as a stranger to this world to save those who had no idea they needed saving!

It is in the hearing of the new covenant only that we become like Jesus, with our minds, clothes, bodies, and spirits glowing in the brightness of His light.

He is the One who loves with endless love and ever-increasing glory! He continually brings good news of His mercy, news of His healing, and news of His unearned and undeserved favor! I invite you today to behold Jesus only and be transfigured by grace Himself!

CHRISTINA PERERA MINISTRIES

It's a relationship!

As you sit at the feet of Jesus daily, hear His voice, commune with Him, pray, and feast on His Word, your life will be transformed.

But we all, with unveiled face, beholding as in a mirror the glory of the Lord, are being transformed into the same image from glory to glory, just as by the Spirit of the Lord.
2 Corinthians 2:18 NKJV

LETS GO DEEP!

Take a few moments and worship the Lord Jesus however you choose. Pray, Sing, or give thanks. Write about it here.

_____

_____

_____

_____

_____

_____

_____

LETS GO DEEPER.

What is Jesus speaking to you? What Bible verses are impacting your heart? Record it here.

_____

_____

_____

_____

_____

_____

Record your response back to Him in prayer here.

_____

_____

_____

_____

_____

_____

_____

_____

_____

Journal about what it means to have a relationship with Him
here.

_____

_____

_____

_____

_____

_____

_____

_____

_____

_____

_____

_____

_____

_____

_____

_____

_____

_____

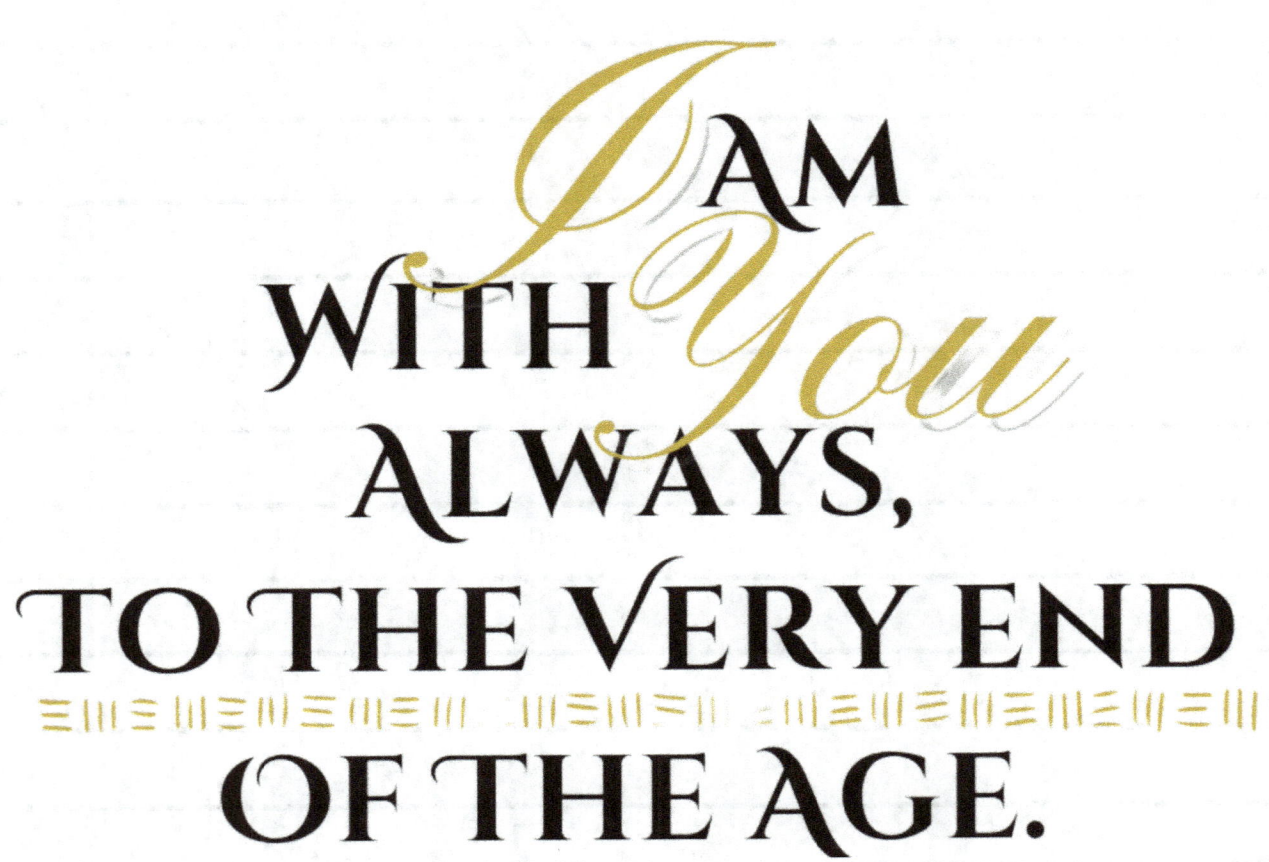

I AM WITH *You* ALWAYS, TO THE VERY END OF THE AGE.

Matthew 28:16 NIV

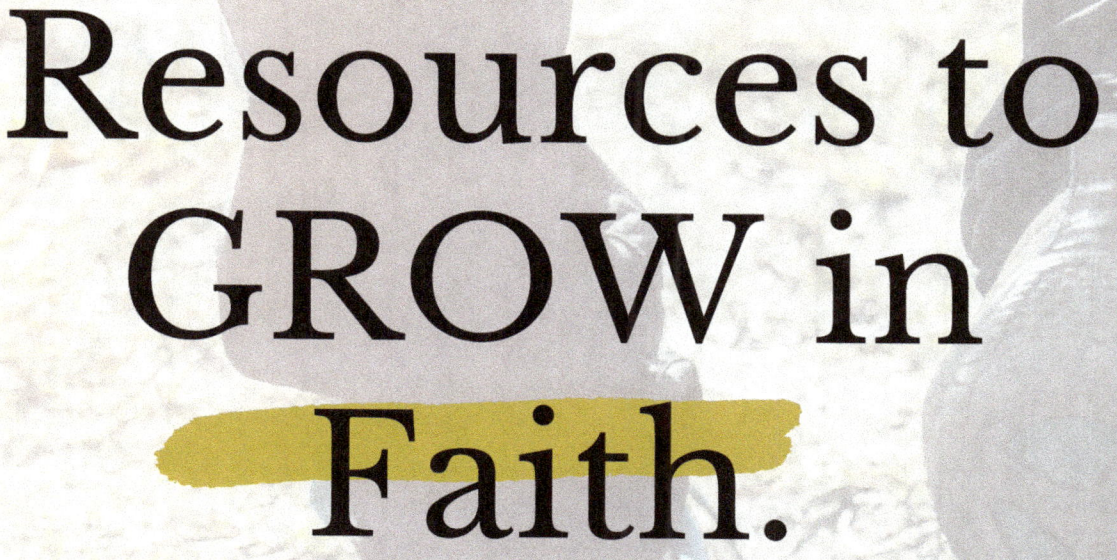

Resources to GROW in ~~Faith.~~

For we are members of His body, of His flesh and of His bones.

Ephesians 5:30 NKJV

PRAYER OF SALVATION

Dear Heavenly Father,

If ask you to forgive me for all my sins. I will be saved if I confess with my mouth that "Jesus is Lord" and believe in my heart that God raised Him from the dead. I believe with my heart and confess with my mouth that Jesus is the Lord and Savior of my life.

Thank you for saving, healing, and delivering me by faith today in the name of Jesus!

I am now a child of God, fully forgiven, fully supplied, and righteous in your eyes Father. I now have righteousness, holiness, and redemption in Christ through His finished work.

I receive the empowering presence of the Holy Spirit and this new creation life by faith. I ask you to baptize me now in the power of the Spirit of God that I may bear the fruit pleasing to you.

In the mighty name of Jesus,
Amen

Notes:

_____

_____

_____

_____

_____

_____

_____

_____

_____

_____

_____

_____

_____

_____

_____

_____

_____

_____

NEXT STEPS TO GROW IN YOUR FAITH

You are now a child of God born into the body of Jesus Christ. You have not been born into a religion but a relationship with the living God! These next steps will help you grow in faith.

- [ ] **GET TO KNOW JESUS THROUGH READING THE BIBLE**
  There are many beautiful translations of the Bible. You can choose the one you can understand best. I recommend the Amplified, New King James, Passion Translation, and New International Version.

- [ ] **READ THE GOSPELS FIRST THEN NEW TESTAMENT LETTERS**
  The gospels are the books of Mathew, Mark, Luke, and John's account of Jesus' life on earth. New Testament letters include Romans, Corinthians, Colossians, Ephesians, and Galatians.

- [ ] **LISTEN TO MESSAGES CENTERED ON JESUS**
  Listen to messages all about the person and work of Jesus, such as *Revealing Jesus with Christina Perera*.

- [ ] **MAKE IT A HABIT TO SPEND TIME WITH JESUS EVERYDAY**
  You can speak to God the way you would a person. He is always with you and willing to listen. Read your Bible and journal what He is speaking/teaching you.

- [ ] **WORSHIP & PRAYER ARE POWERFUL**
  Anytime you worship God, His presence manifests around you, driving out all darkness and fighting your every enemy. Singing, praying, and giving thanks are all forms of worship.

- [ ] **GET CONNECTED TO A BODY OF BELIEVERS**
  Join a local church, online organization, or ministry such as CPM. Staying connected to other believers will help you grow in faith.

- [ ] **SPREAD THE LOVE**
  Become a volunteer and actively engage your community by sharing the good news of what Jesus has done in your life!

Notes:

_____

_____

_____

_____

_____

_____

_____

_____

_____

_____

_____

_____

_____

_____

_____

_____

_____

_____

Hey! I'm "Christina"

[I]s my heart's greatest desire to encourage you in your new relationship with Jesus. As a 5- fold minister, [r]ivalist, author, and speaker with a fiery passion for Jesus that spreads like wildfire, I carry the revelation [of] the gospel of Jesus Christ. I long to bring the body of Christ into the fullness of the finished work of Jesus [and] see each one of us reach a hurting world with love. It is a great honor to encourage others in the [go]odness of God.

[I s]incerely hope this New Believer Workbook has blessed your relationship with God and deepened your [wa]lk with Him. I would love to keep in touch and continue encouraging you in the things of God!

[W]e would love to hear how this workbook has blessed you. Please leave a review on Amazon to help others [kn]ow how it has blessed you. You can follow us on social media at @christinapereraministres on Facebook [& I]nstagram. Listen to hear more about our beautiful Savior Jesus on *Revealing Jesus With Christina Perera* [wh]erever you get your podcasts.

LET'S KEEP IN TOUCH

JOIN THE MOVEMENT
TO SPREAD
THE EXTRAVAGANT
LOVE OF GOD!

Christina Perera Ministries is passionate about unity in the body of Christ, strengthening His body, and fulfilling the Great Commission!

Join our mailing list, volunteer, and listen to Revealing Jesus wherever you get your podcasts. Find more resources to grow in faith at www.christinaperera.org

You can help fulfill the Great Commission and reach others with the good news of Jesus!

Together, we will go into all the world and share the good news of Jesus.